$ 2.95

The Developing Child

Recent decades have witnessed unprecedented advances in research on human development. Each book in The Developing Child series reflects the importance of this research as a resource for enhancing children's well-being. It is the purpose of the series to make this resource available to that increasingly large number of people who are responsible for raising a new generation. We hope that these books will provide rich and useful information for parents, educators, child-care professionals, students of developmental psychology, and all others concerned with childhood.

Jerome Bruner, University of Oxford
Michael Cole, Rockefeller University
Barbara Lloyd, University of Sussex
Series Editors

The Perceptual
World
of the Child

T. G. R. Bower

Harvard University Press
Cambridge, Massachusetts
1977

Library of Congress Cataloging in Publication Data
Bower, T   G   R   1941-
  The perceptual world of the child.

  (The Developing child)
  Bibliography: p.
  Includes index.
  1. Perception in children.   I. Title.   II. Series.
BF723.P36B68   155.4'13   77-8316
ISBN 0-674-66193-1
ISBN 0-674-66192-3 pbk.

Contents

1 / Perceptions of the Child's Perceptual World

This is a book about the ways in which the developing child perceives the world around him, and about his growing ability to make sense of what he perceives.

Perception ordinarily refers to any process by which we gain immediate awareness of what is happening outside ourselves. The key word here is "immediate." We can only gain immediate information about that part of the world that directly impinges on our senses. The world we perceive is the world that we see, hear, smell, taste, and touch. My perceptual world at the moment is a room about twenty feet by twenty feet, normally furnished, rather silent. Through an open window I can smell something faintly sweet and hear a distant rumbling. This is a pretty restricted perceptual environment, and becomes even more so when I focus on the page of yellow paper on which I am writing these words. I could make it less restricted by getting up and walking outside. But as an adult I have other resources as well. My world is not only perceptual. I have memory and knowledge. I can remember that the smell in my room comes from the jasmine outside in the garden, and I "hear" the rumbling noises outside as the sounds of a passing car. I can, to some extent, live in the future by thinking about what I am going to do. I can use TV, newspapers, and books to transport myself to worlds I will never perceive directly.

The newborn baby does not have these resources. He has few memories and probably no thoughts of the future. He lives in a completely perceptual world. But perception is also less useful to the baby than to us because he cannot actively control it as we can. He can refuse to look at things, as we can, but he cannot go out and look for things. If the baby is hungry, naturally he cannot look for food in the refrigerator, because he cannot walk and also because he does not know that food is inside refrigerators. Lack of knowledge means that the baby cannot use his perceptual system in the way that adults can.

All our knowledge of the world comes through our senses, initially. It is by means of his sensory apparatus that the baby comes to know what his mother looks like, what food of certain colors tastes like, and so on. This sensory information is stored and transformed into a system of knowledge that in turn can direct the use of the perceptual system. Some psychologists argue that knowledge actually changes the way we see things, but this idea is very difficult to evaluate. Does a refrigerator look different once we know that it probably contains food? A difficult question, perhaps impossible to answer. What we can say, however, is that the *meaning*, or significance, of the sight of the refrigerator changes once we know it is a cold compartment in which to store food. Without this knowledge, the sight of a refrigerator may signify nothing more than a shiny surface or a large rectangular object. In a sense, then, the world of the very small child must be relatively meaningless. Before the perceptual world takes on adult meaning, the baby has to learn a great deal about the world, a great deal about what can be done with what. Much of the knowledge that informs our perceptions is not available to the baby. I say "much," not "all," because there is evidence that some knowledge does not have to be learned. For example, the baby seems to come into the world already knowing an amazing amount about human beings, a surprising fact that I will discuss later in some detail.

Not so long ago many scholars argued that the baby's perceptual world is completely bare of meaning, even the kind of meaning involved in *seeing* that a stone is *hard.* Some scholars delighted in pointing out that "hardness" belongs to the sense of touch; only by touching can we know that a stone is hard. When we say that we see something is hard, the argument goes, we are really saying that we see something we have learned is hard because we have already touched it. If this were true, then very young babies would not know which things are hard and which are not. Many psychologists have written about the baby as if he lived in a visual world of insubstantial pictures, lacking any meaning. His visual world has been characterized as totally separated from the world of touch, the world of hearing, the world of smell. The baby was supposed to be unable to coordinate information from two or more senses, something that we adults take totally for granted. Worse still, the baby was supposed to lack any constancy in his perceptual world, which would mean that perception of the size, the color, the position, and even the existence of objects would fluctuate depending upon the sensory quality of the environment. Consider what it would mean if babies lacked the most elementary constancies, such as *visual position constancy.* When you look at an array of objects, each object is projected onto the retina of your eye in an orderly way, and from there to your brain, resulting in perception of those objects in that particular place. When you move your eye, every one of these objects is projected to a different part of the retina, and from there to a different part of the brain. Despite these changes, you see the objects as retaining a constant position. Our perceptual system adjusts for the eye movement to yield position constancy. If the baby lacks position constancy, as many have argued, his world would indeed be a flickering, evanescent whirl, filled with shadows, swinging around in no predictable way.

It is important to note that arguments of this kind were advanced largely by philosophers sitting in their proverbial armchairs. Their "data" were not garnered from observing babies. Despite the lack of evidence, the very antiquity of these ideas has given them respectability, and supporting arguments have been offered by scientists of various persuasions. Evolutionary biologists have long sought a reason for the extended duration of human childhood. The young of most other species are ready to live independently long before human children are. Some have argued that a lengthy infancy is required because the human is born with a nonfunctional brain (and therefore a nonfunctional perceptual system) that must be trained to function through experience. During this training period, the immature organism requires care and nurturing; hence the need for a long childhood. This argument ignores the general rule that the more capable a species is in adulthood, the more capable is the newborn of that species. Unless the human species is a glaring exception, this rule would lead us to expect high capability in the human newborn. Of course, human infants do not look very capable, and neurologists have pointed out that the brain of the baby is different from the adult's: the cells are smaller and the connections between them poorly insulated. But it would be strange to conclude from this that the brain of the baby does not work at all. In the first place, we simply do not know enough about the relationship between brain structure and function to draw any such conclusion. Second, and again this will become clearer later, it is obvious that even the brain of a newborn baby supports some truly remarkable perceptual abilities.

These old ideas about the child's perceptions grow out of general philosophical and biological considerations. They are plausible and familiar, but they advance hypotheses about the capacities of the newborn child that are not based on direct examination of the newborn's capacities. Our task, then, is to take a direct look at the perceptual world of the young child, a world that must certainly be different from ours, but nonetheless one we can learn a great deal about through carefully arranged observations.

2 / Some Complex Effects of Simple Growth

Since there are some differences between the physical structure of adult sensory systems and those of the baby, there are inevitable differences between our perceptions of the world and the baby's perceptions of the same world.

We have six sensory systems. The first five correspond to the senses of touch, taste, smell, hearing, and sight. The sixth is proprioception, the sense that tells us where the mobile parts of our bodies are in relation to all the rest— where our hands are in relation to one another, to the head, the trunk, and so on. All of these senses have the same surface structure, consisting of specialized peripheral receptors connected to the brain by a network of nerves.

The receptors for smell line the nose, just as those for taste line the mouth. There is not much difference between adults and babies in terms of these receptor systems, save that the baby has fewer receptors than we do and presumably cannot make the fine discriminations we can. But changes in body size do make a difference that is easily overlooked if we concentrate only on the receptors themselves.

The sense of touch arises from a complex system of receptors in the skin. The main difference between us and a baby is that an adult's skin surface, of course, is very much

6

larger than a baby's. A point on the adult chest will be a certain distance from the breastbone, some distance from the shoulder, and so on. For the baby, the relationship of any specific point on the body to the rest of the body changes tremendously with growth. This may be unimportant. But the rapid growth of the baby's skin could mean that he is generally uncertain about the locus of a touch on any part of his skin surface.

The same growth-induced uncertainty might interfere with accurate proprioception. The proprioceptive receptors lie in our joints and respond basically to the angle between two bones. Whether this information can accurately tell the baby where his hand is, for example, is not clear, because his arm is always growing. Can the baby know the length of his own arm and monitor changes in it? The answer to this apparently simple question is not obvious, as we shall see later.

As far as the basic physical aspects of the ear's structure are concerned, the baby's ear is pretty much like the adult's, except that it is smaller. The size difference produces a difference in the range of sounds that the baby can hear as compared to the adult; the baby can hear sounds at a higher pitch, such as high-pitched whistles, better than we can. But this is not a great difference. The most significant difference between baby and adult is not *within* the ear at all. It is the distance *between* the two ears, which is important in sound localization. Because we have two ears that are some distance apart, sounds from a source on our right or left will strike one ear before the other, while sounds from sources straight ahead will arrive at both ears simultaneously. The difference in time of arrival relates exactly to deviation from the position straight ahead. However, this difference is naturally determined by the distance between the two ears as well as by the position of the sound source. The problem for the baby is that the distance at birth is much less than it will be when he is an adult, as (1) shows. What does this imply? The signal specifying a sound source straight ahead does not change during growth. Similarly, a source on the right will always stimulate the right ear before the left ear, and a source on the left will always stimulate the left ear before the right. There is thus no reason why a baby should not have built-in mechanisms to signal these source positions. However, *precise* position to right or left depends on information that changes continually during growth. It is quite possible that there are built-in mechanisms that would handle these problems, too. Based on what we know about sensory structures, though, it seems reasonable to expect that the baby will have to learn the significance of a precise time-of-arrival difference and, having learned it, will have to relearn it continuously as his head gets bigger.

Finally we come to the most complex sensory system,

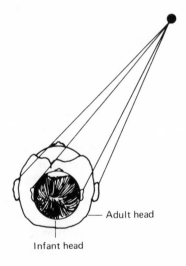

1. *Because the infant's head is so much smaller than the adult's, the time difference between the arrival of a sound at one ear and at the other is much less.*

Adult head

Infant head

the eye and its associated neural structures. The eye is an extremely intricate and complex organ (2). Light enters the eye through the cornea, passes through the anterior chamber and thence through the pupil to the lens. The lens is a soft transparent tissue that can stretch out and get thinner or shorten and thicken, thus focusing the rays of light and enabling images of objects at different distances to be seen clearly. The lens focuses the light on the retina, which is the thin membrane covering the posterior surface of the eyeball. The nerve cells in the retina itself are sensitive to spots of light. Each nerve cell at the next level of analysis in the brain receives inputs from a number of these retinal nerve cells and responds best to lines or long edges in particular orientations. Numbers of these nerve cells feed into

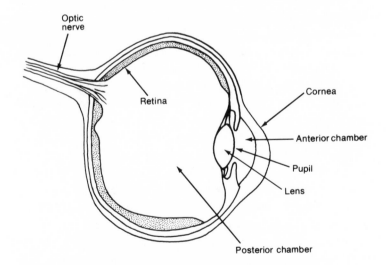

2. *The adult eye. Light is focused by the lens onto the retina, where cells that are sensitive to different wavelengths and patterns of light pass signals along the optic nerve to the brain.*

the next level, where nerve cells are sensitive to movement of lines in particular orientations in particular directions. There are other levels that seem sensitive to size, and still others that respond to specific differences in the signals from the two eyes. The important thing for us to keep in mind in trying to understand the child's perceptual world is that in all species yet studied, particularly in those species close to man, these structures in the visual system are present at birth. There is every reason to believe that the same is true of the human newborn. At birth the baby should have a very efficient visual system, because the structures just mentioned allow him to register a great deal of useful information.

There are some effects of growth, however, that may limit the kind of information that the infant's visual system can register. The basic structures are the same, but there are some significant differences between the adult and the infant eye. First of all, the lens of the eye, which can change its shape in adults to permit precise focusing of objects at different distances, does not change in infants. This means that the image projected onto the infant's retina is somewhat blurrier than that typically projected onto the adult's; at worst, the infant might not see some things that are perfectly visible to an adult.

Moreover, the infant eye is somewhat shorter or shallower than the adult eye (3), which means that the size of the retinal image produced by a specific object at a specific distance will be much less. The perceived size of any object is related to the size of this image. The size-perception mechanism, which translates image size into a representation of object size, is thus subject to growth changes. The baby should be able to see when two objects are the same size, or when one is bigger than the other. However, if required to use *absolute* size information, he has difficulties.

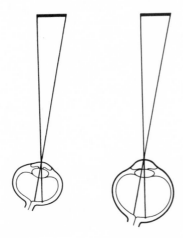

3. *The same object will project a small image on the shallow infant eye and a larger one on the deeper adult eye.*

For example, suppose the baby wants to reach out and grasp an object he sees. His perception of the object's size, based on the image's size, will probably not be accurate enough for this. Indeed, since the size of the object must be matched to the size of the hand, which is itself growing, there are two sources of error in the perceptual components of this act, errors that most likely require learning if they are to be overcome.

Size perception, of course, depends on more than image size. The size of the image produced by an object of a given size changes with distance (4). Adults perceive size as constant despite such changes in distance and consequent changes in image size. This means that adults are coordinating information about distance and information about image size to provide a representation of real size. So in order to understand perception of size, we must also know something about perception of distance. Can babies be reasonably expected to perceive it?

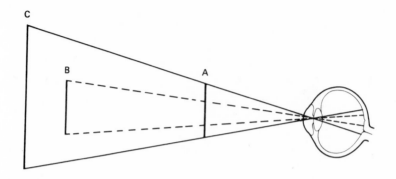

4. *Size constancy. Though the retinal images of A and C are the same, an adult actually sees A and B as the same size, and both of them smaller than C.*

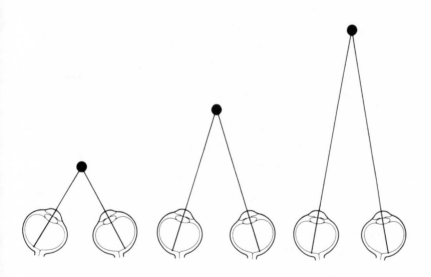

5. *Judging distance. As an object approaches, the eyes converge.*

There are many sources of information about distance. One comes from the fact that we have binocular vision. As we look at objects at different distances, the angle between our two eyes changes, as shown in (5). But the angle is obviously dependent on the distance between the two eyes as well as the distance from the eyes to the object, and the former distance changes drastically during development. These consequences of growth suggest that the baby will have to learn to use the angle of convergence between eyes and objects as a source of information about distance.

The fact that we have two eyes also gives us a source of

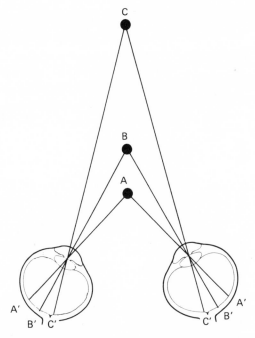

6. *Judging which object is closer. The image on one retina is the opposite of the image on the other.*

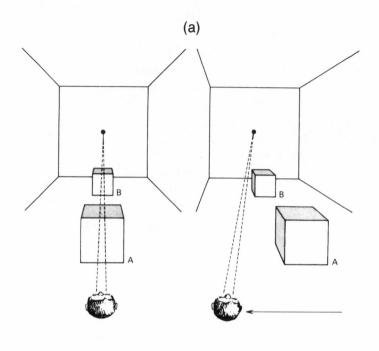

(a)

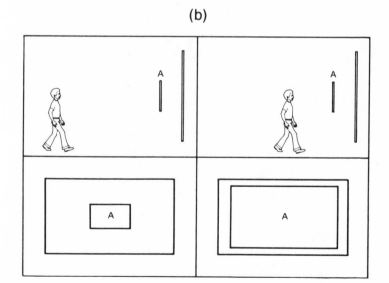

(b)

(c)

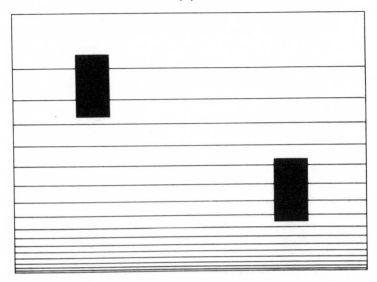

7. *Three sources of information about distance.*
(a) *Motion parallax. If you move your head to the left, a closer object appears to move farther and faster to the right than a farther one does.*
(b) *Optical expansion. The retinal image of an object expands as you approach. The closer the object, the greater the expansion. Rectangle A expands more rapidly as the boy approaches.*
(c) *Textural occlusion. One object is higher in the frame and so is seen as farther away. That object also occludes more of the background texture and so seems farther away.*

information about relative distance that is *not* growth-dependent. That source is binocular disparity. A simple example of this distance cue is shown by holding up your thumbs one in front of the other at different distances from the eyes. If you shut one eye and then the other, the non-corresponding distances are clearly seen. The perceived distance between the thumbs varies with both the distance of the thumbs from the eyes and from each other. Suppose we look at an object three feet away. Any object closer than that, or any object that is farther away, is projected onto noncorresponding points on our two eyes. The closer object produces an input that is the exact opposite of the pattern produced by the farther object, as shown in (6).

There are many other sources of information about distance that are also not growth-dependent. Three of them are motion parallax, optical expansion, and textural occlusion (7). Motion parallax depends on no more than the ability to move the head. Optical expansion depends on object movement or self-movement. Textural occlusion seems to depend on assumptions about the constancy of texture in the world. The texture of the world indoors is different from that of the world outdoors. Outdoors a plowed field is very different from a beach, and both are very different from a paved sidewalk. Textural occlusion can be used as a distance cue in all of these situations, but only with the benefit of some knowledge about specific textures. The other two sources of information do not require such knowledge and so could be used by the infant.

In sum, there are a number of reasons to suspect that newborn babies can perceive distance even if they cannot do it quite as well as adults. In the next chapter we will see that there is some direct experimental evidence to support this suspicion.

3 / Perceiving Things, Perceiving People

Babies are very competent, although they are rarely very cooperative with those who seek to examine their competencies. In part, this lack of cooperation stems from limitations that are not direct reflections of their ability to perceive. For example, newborn babies are not awake for very long—six minutes is about as long a period of full wakefulness as one can expect. Also, small babies suffer from postural limitations. If lying flat on his back, the baby must use his head and arms in order to maintain his balance (8). Lastly, the only way we can induce a baby to cooperate with us is to engage his interest, and that's not easy to do. What we find interesting may not be interesting to a baby. The baby's world is not our world. In order to interest a baby we must find ways to enter into his way of seeing the world. This requires patient observation and no small amount of imagination. In effect, we will see that investigations of the infant's perceptual world amount to a series of educated guesses. Each experiment advances our knowledge as it confirms or disconfirms a guess, bringing us closer to viewing the world through the eyes, ears, taste, and touch of the infant.

What, then, is the perceptual world of the newborn child? How well does he organize the information flooding in on his senses? At the outset it must be said that the

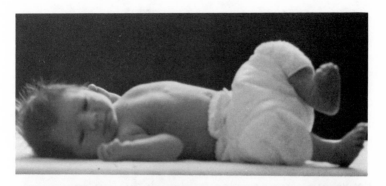

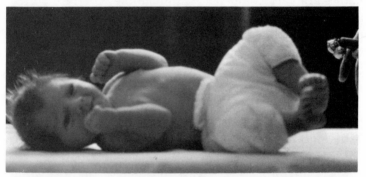

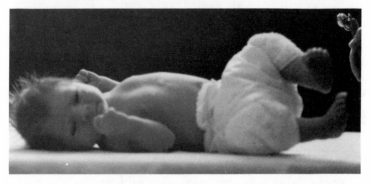

8. *A newborn has to use his arms to keep his balance (top). If he moves his arms (middle), he is unable to maintain his position except by propping himself on his arm (bottom).*

amount of organization is amazing. Even the biological resources outlined in the last chapter seem inadequate to explain the capacities the newborn demonstrates. Consider
the simple sense of touch. The skin is a growing organ, and
the specific receptors in the skin change their position during growth. Still the newborn baby seems to know what
part of his skin is being touched and will demonstrate this
knowledge if the touch is irritating. J. B. Watson long ago
demonstrated that a newborn can remove an irritant from
his nose with his hand or get rid of an irritant on one leg
with his other foot.[1] These abilities are astonishing, con-
sidering the growth problems of the skin and the growth
problems posed to the proprioceptive system by changes in
arm and leg length. Seemingly trivial, they imply an impressive amount of inbuilt organization.

The most specialized skin sense is taste. Babies prefer
sweet substances, just as most adults do, and will take
them in preference to more nutritious, less sweet things,
such as breast milk. Beyond this, not much is known about
taste.

What of smell? Babies certainly show preferences for
certain odors over others, finding some nauseating. They
can localize odor sources and, very soon after birth, will
smoothly turn away from odors they find unpleasant.
Babies are also able to "switch off" smells so that they are
no longer registered. This ability, known as "habituation,"
is extremely important in the perceptual development of
all the sensory systems. Habituation is not simple fatigue
of the sensory receptors. What appears to happen is this:
as a smell, or any other stimulus, is repeated, an internal
representation or schema of the stimulus is built up in the
baby's perceptual system. After a while, any stimulus that
matches the schema is automatically blocked and does not
reach awareness. This kind of specific blocking process is

shown clearly in one experiment where babies were presented with a mixture of two odoriferous chemicals. At first they turned toward the odor each time it was presented. After a few trials, however, they had habituated to the source and no longer showed any response. They were then presented with a new odor, which was made by substituting water for one of the chemicals in the original mixture; the total concentration was thus weaker than before. If habituation were simply a matter of fatigue, the babies should have been even less likely to respond to the new odor than to the original stronger concentration of odors. What in fact happened was that the new, weaker stimulus elicited a strong response from the babies. Habituation, then, is not simple sensory fatigue; it must result from the construction of an internal schema that is used to exclude specific stimuli.

Hearing is a relatively unresearched area, but there is one study of particular relevance. Michael Wertheimer studied auditory localization in a baby only a few moments after birth.[2] In the last chapter I argued that the newborn baby probably can tell when a sound source is straight ahead and when it is not, and that he can localize a sound source to his right or to his left without being able to determine its precise location. As Wertheimer's results show, this turns out to be about right. But the interesting part of Wertheimer's study was the method he used to prove it. Wertheimer guessed that the baby's eye movements might give a clue to his perception of a sound source, and indeed he found in his experiment that the baby looked to the right when the sound was on the right, to the left when the sound was on the left. Similar observations have been made by other investigators, although their subjects were hours rather than seconds old. These findings not only show auditory localization but also an expectation that there will be something to *look at*, a source for the sound. Here we seem to have found a simple form of intersensory coordination which is present at birth.

The visual capacities of the newborn are much better developed than folklore about infants might lead us to expect. Because of the importance of vision, these capacities are also well studied relative to the other senses. There has been a long-standing controversy over whether newborns see the world in depth or perceive it initially as a flat picture on the surface of the eye—much as a touch is felt on the skin. But it now seems fairly clear that a baby's initial visual experience is three-dimensional. Infants can pick up the position of an object in three-dimensional space as well as changes of position in space. One way the infant gives evidence of this ability is by showing appropriate defensive responses to approaching objects.

My own research in this area was stimulated by pediatrician Mary Sheridan. She told me that the defensive response to a real object moving toward a baby's face differentiates blind and sighted babies: the sighted babies respond, but the blind babies do not. In a sense, this was a surprising result. Since the object used in the test is a real object, its movement displaces air, which can be felt by both blind and sighted babies. But only the sighted babies show the defensive reaction. Apparently it is the sight of the approaching object which triggers the response. To test this more thoroughly, my colleagues and I arranged three laboratory settings to present object movement with air movement, air movement by itself, and object movement by itself. Since the defensive response in its full form is difficult to elicit consistently because few babies have strength to maintain the necessary body and head position, we supported the babies so as to prevent large head movements as we used a pressure transducer to record the defensive response as any backward pressure of the head.

The first experimental condition, object movement with air movement, produced a very clear defensive response from the babies (9). Air movement by itself produced a completely different response, with no measurable head retraction. But visible object movement by itself, without air movement, did produce the defensive response. The response was somewhat weaker than when air movement was present, but still clearly discernible. Clearly, the visi-

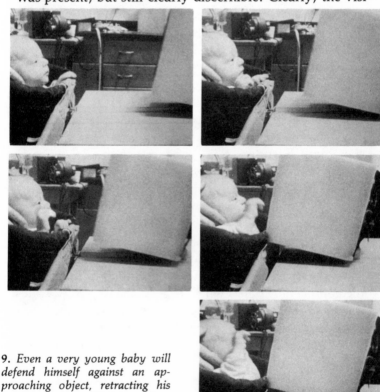

9. *Even a very young baby will defend himself against an approaching object, retracting his head and raising his arms. How does he know without experience that defense is necessary?*

ble approach of a moving object is important in setting off the defensive response. So, the infant must be capable of detecting the changing positions of visible objects moving in space.

The defensive response has been used to reveal other aspects of space perception in very small babies. For example, there is some evidence that babies can distinguish specific distances rather than simply changes of distance. If one moves objects toward babies, the defensive response will not occur until the objects are within a certain critical distance. The distance is unaffected by the size of the object, even though a larger object farther away produces a retinal image of the same size as a smaller but closer object.

The same response has also been used to show that babies are very sensitive to the direction from which objects approach. An object approaching on a direct hit path will elicit a defensive response, whereas an object approaching on a miss path will not (10).

There is another unstated capacity that may underpin these defensive responses. The defensive reaction does not appear to be a simple reflex like the knee jerk. It is both more elaborate and less automatic. Indeed it looks rather as if this reaction is controlled by higher cortical centers which make the complex calculations required to determine that the object is hard, on a collision course, and potentially painful to contact. Jane Dunkeld compared babies' responses to an approaching object with their responses to an approaching hole. In terms of contour expansion the two are identical, and yet it was only the approaching object that elicited defensive responses. An object, of course, is perceptually different from an aperture (11). Newborns seem able to pick up these differences and seem to realize that one perception signifies emptiness and the other hardness and solidity. Hardness is a property detected by the

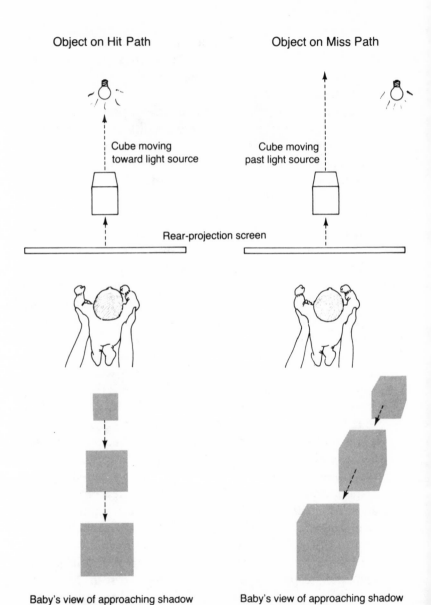

Object on Hit Path | Object on Miss Path

Cube moving toward light source | Cube moving past light source

Rear-projection screen

Baby's view of approaching shadow | Baby's view of approaching shadow

10. *How a baby is presented with objects apparently on hit or miss paths. He can judge quite finely between the two situations.*

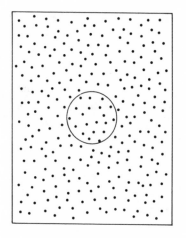 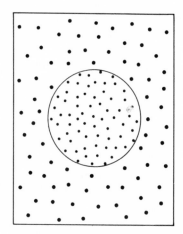

11(a). *An approaching aperture*

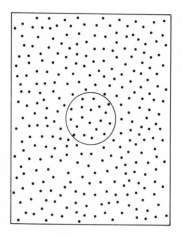 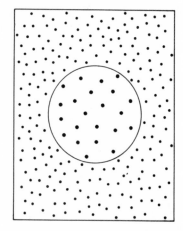

11(b). *An approaching object.*

Notice how the grain increases in the approaching object but not in the approaching hole.

sense of touch. The fact that the babies can perceive a visible event as signifying potential tangibility and hardness is yet another indication that they live in a unified perceptual world, with some degree of intersensory coordination.

The defensive response to approaching objects has also been used to demonstrate one of the major limitations of the immature perceptual system. It appears that while the baby can take in information about events in the world, the rate at which he processes this information is very slow. In the approaching-object situation, the speed of approach can be so rapid that the baby seems to perceive nothing. Apparently, a fast approach puts too much information into a baby's visual system at one time for him to be able to handle it, so that, in effect, nothing is perceived.

Other aspects of the visual perception of space have been explored by making use of the very primitive reaching behavior of newborn babies. In order to study reaching, it is necessary to support the baby so that his head and arms are free to move and are not required for support; we can then present objects for him to reach for (12). The accuracy of reaching can be cautiously taken as one indicator of the accuracy of visual localization. There is of course always the problem that errors could occur either in the proprioceptive perception of hand and arm position or in the execution of the movement. But, as I mentioned in the last chapter, the infant's tactual localization is quite good. In any event, the data show that small babies can locate the position of an object to the right or the left with an accuracy such that the bulk of their reaches lands either on the object or within half an inch of it—which is not unimpressive. As far as distance is concerned, babies are quite ready to reach for objects that are out of reach but much less ready than they are to reach for objects within reach. They

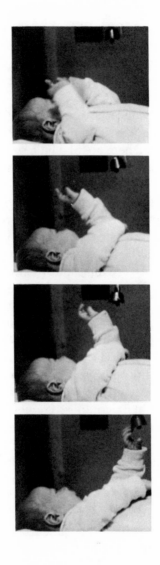

12. *Though coordinating hand and eye is a complex maneuver, a newborn can reach for a toy with great accuracy.*

also seem to learn quite quickly that objects at a particular distance are unattainable. Again note that there is an implicit intersensory coordination between sight and touch at work here. The baby acts as if he knows that an object he sees can be touched.

So far we have concerned ourselves with the newborn's perceptions of the physical world. Although the accomplishments revealed here are of a high order, they pale into insignificance beside the precision of the newborn's perceptions of people.

There have been a number of recent studies of imitation in newborn infants. In one, a baby is propped up face to face opposite his mother. She begins to stick her tongue out at him. Usually the baby stares raptly at his mother's face and tongue for a while, and then begins to stick his tongue back out. Suppose the mother then shifts to fluttering her eyelashes at the baby. The baby will quickly flutter his eyelashes back at her. If she next starts to open her mouth, the baby will follow suit, shifting to imitative mouth-opening as well (13).

Consider just how complex an achievement this is. First of all the baby must pick out the relevant portion of his mother's face. That is complex enough, but recognizing that his mother's tongue is a tongue is even more complex. The baby recognizes that his own tongue, which he can only know by the feel of it in his mouth and between his lips, matches his mother's tongue, which he sees—and this is truly astonishing. It implies that the baby has a perceptual image of parts of his own body which is elaborate enough to allow him to be able to identify parts of his own body with parts of other people's bodies. This is intersensory coordination with a vengeance! Remember that we are talking about newborn babies, who have never examined themselves in mirrors or done any of the self-dis-

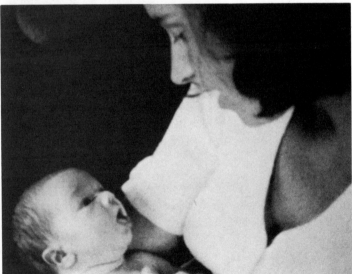

13. *A six-day-old baby imitates his mother as she opens her mouth. He knows that part of her (which he can see) is equivalent to part of himself (which he has never seen but can feel), and he knows how to perform the same act.*

covering things that adults can do. This capacity for imitation has implications well beyond perception. Among other things, it suggests that the newborn baby recognizes some identity between himself and the people who take care of him; apparently he feels himself to be a member of the human race right from the start.

We have been concerned with capacities that allow the newborn to begin organizing the world as soon as he comes into it. There is one other capacity present at birth which has the most potent organizing influence of all: the ability to perceive connections, which underlies the ability to learn. There has been controversy over whether or not newborns can learn, but now some even claim that humans learn more efficiently in the newborn period than at any later age. In one classic study by E. R. Siqueland and L. P. Lipsitt, the following set of connections was arranged: whenever a bell sounded and the baby turned his head to the right, he would receive a few drops of sugar water; whenever a buzzer sounded, the baby was not to turn his head.[3] The structure of the experiment was therefore

$$bell \rightarrow turn\ head\ right \rightarrow sugar\ water$$
$$buzzer \rightarrow don't\ turn\ head$$

Babies on the first day of life were able to master this structure. Furthermore, when the contingencies were reversed so that the structure became

$$bell \rightarrow don't\ turn\ head$$
$$buzzer \rightarrow turn\ head\ right \rightarrow sugar\ water$$

the babies were able to adapt to the reversal very quickly, indeed, more quickly than any nonhuman primate would have.

This is simple learning of what goes with what. But it produces changes in perceptual organization within the first few weeks of life. A striking instance of this kind of change occurs in the area of social perception. Genevieve Carpenter set up an experiment in which babies were shown the following situations at the age of two weeks: (1) mother, speaking to them in her own voice, (2) strange female, speaking to them in her own voice, (3) mother, speaking to them in female stranger's voice, (4) stranger, speaking to them in mother's voice.[4] The babies found the first of these situations the most attractive. They looked more often at the mother than they looked at the stranger in the second presentation, showing that even at this age they can differentiate between mother and stranger. Even more interesting, they did not like the third and fourth presentations at all, actively turning away from the demonstration and trying to avoid looking at the bizarre combination of sights and sounds. The only way the babies could know that (3) and (4) are bizarre events is by learning that their mother's face goes with their mother's voice. The speed with which they learn this association should warn us that they are probably making similarly rapid organizational associations all the time.

So the infant begins life with an impressive ability to make sense of his perceptions of people and things and his remarkable capacity for learning suggests that his perceptual world is becoming increasingly meaningful at a rapid rate. But, as any parent might suspect, these surprising capabilities are not without their limitations. It is the precise nature of these limitations that will concern us next.

4 / How Much Can Babies Take In?

Although the newborn has a remarkably capable perceptual system, there appear to be severe limits on the amount of information he can take in at one time. These limitations persist into infancy.

One of my own learning experiments may serve to illustrate the way these limitations work. Babies were trained to respond to the pattern shown at the top of (14) for a reward, which was a peek-a-boo. When the babies were responding consistently, they were shown each of the bits of the pattern separately, and they responded just as readily to the bits as to the whole thing. They didn't seem to notice the difference. What this suggests to me is that the babies were unable to attend to the whole pattern as it was presented, because of their limited information-processing capacity. What they saw at any one time was a circle, or a cross, or a pair of dots. When they were shown the bits separately, as far as they were concerned they were seeing just what they had been trained to respond to, and so they responded. By about three months of age, infants stopped responding to the parts of the pattern as if the parts were identical to the whole. Apparently, by this age, infants are able to attend to all the information in a simple pattern.

More complicated patterns, such as a human face, may take longer to grasp as a whole. Some of the evidence on

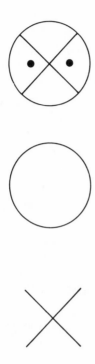

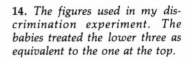

14. *The figures used in my discrimination experiment. The babies treated the lower three as equivalent to the one at the top.*

this point stems from the many attempts to find out what stimuli produce smiling in infants. When babies begin to smile at people, at about six weeks of age, it is clear that a whole face is not required to elicit the response. Two dark blobs, side by side, will do. Movement of a contour that is roughly face-shaped will also elicit smiling. By the age of three months, more of the face has become important, and there is evidence that the whole-face pattern is beginning to be picked up around this time. For instance, an upright face will elicit more smiling than a face turned on its side or upside down. Not all of the face is important, since a face without a mouth will still get a smile. But the absence of a complete facial contour is quite critical by this age. A face cut away below the nose will elicit aversion rather than smiling. At five months the mouth must be there—indeed, a smiling mouth is more likely to elicit smiling than a non-smiling mouth from this age on. It seems quite clear that the baby can now perceive all of the parts of a face at once. Further support for this view comes from the baby's growing ability to differentiate between people and between the moods of any one person. By the age of eight months, a baby can respond to subtle facial indicators of mood showing on the face of any adult who approaches him. It seems perfectly possible that it is the growth in information-handling capacity that allows the baby to process all of these extra features.

The limited capacity of the baby is also involved in developmental changes that lie on the borders between perception and action. One example is the development of reaching skills. Accurate reaching, of course, depends on correct perceptual localization of an object. It also involves correct perceptual localization of the hand. The motor component consists of transporting the hand from its perceived location to the perceived location of the object. If the perceptual system is used to monitor this transport, perception is involved in yet a third way. So any "perceptual-motor" act, like reaching, is far more perceptual than motor. There is some evidence that babies under five months have difficulties with this perceptual aspect of motor behavior. In reaching, it appears that babies have particular difficulties in monitoring hand transport, which shows up as an interruption of reaching whenever the hand enters the visual field. The hand competes with the object for attention, to such an extent that the act of reaching can be disrupted. The baby will simply stop the act of reaching and stare fixedly at his hand. After growing bored with the hand, he will notice the object again. His reach may be interrupted yet again when the hand enters the central portion of his visual field. Even when this phase of alternating attention is over, he still cannot attend to hand and object simultaneously. However, it requires some experimental trickery to show this. This involves having the baby reach while wearing wedge prisms (15, 16). Wedge prisms displace the light coming from an object so that the object appears to one side of its actual location. When babies of less than five months reach for an object while wearing wedge prisms, they aim for the place where the object is seen to be rather than to its actual place. The amazing thing is that they miss it and cannot correct their reach. They simply pull their hands back, try again, miss again. This can go on for some time, while the baby becomes more and more frustrated. Babies of seven months, by contrast, are not affected at all by wearing wedge prisms and they capture an object with ease. Detailed analysis of their reaches shows that these older babies misperceive the position of objects just as the younger babies do. The first part of the reach is on a mistaken path. However, as soon as the hand enters the visual field, its trajectory is corrected and brought smoothly to the object. It is this double attention, to both hand position and object position, that seems to be beyond the scope of the younger babies, who do not have the informational resources to monitor the position of the hand in relation to the object.

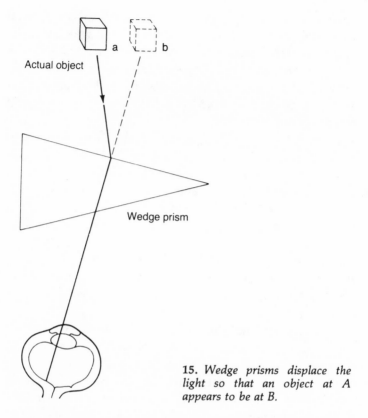

Actual object

Wedge prism

15. *Wedge prisms displace the light so that an object at A appears to be at B.*

Information-processing limitations are characteristic of the developing child, and affect performance for years. I will mention one last instance from a seminatural experimental situation. A baby is shown a desirable toy placed on a table, under one of three cups—say the one on the baby's left. The cups are out of reach so the baby has to move around the table to get at them. Babies of less than eighteen months will do this, but once in position will reach out to take the cup on their left, rather than the correct cup, which is now on their right. The division of attention between walking and watching the cups seems to

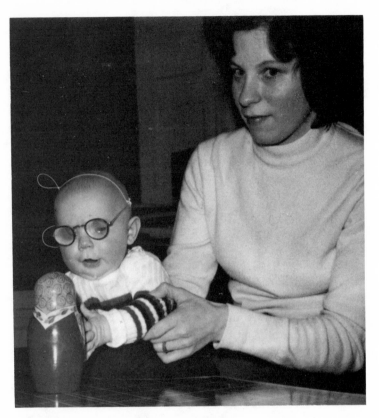

16. *A baby wearing wedge prisms.*

be too much for them. The task immediately becomes much easier if the table is rotated so that the baby doesn't have to move. Again it seems that the information required for moving competes within the perceptual system with the information required to monitor cup position.

So far, I have been emphasizing the limitations on the amount of information the infant can handle. But how does his perceptual system change so that large amounts of information can be processed? Part of the change is undoubtedly the result of growth. The nerve cells within the perceptual system grow and increase in number. The nerve fibers carrying information to the brain, as well as those that circulate information within the brain, grow thicker so that they carry messages faster. The fibers also become better insulated so that the messages carried in adjacent channels do not interfere with one another.

This is growth and, like body growth, which requires physical exercise, the growth within the perceptual system requires exercise from stimulus inputs. The brains of animals that are denied such inputs simply do not grow and, in fact, may degenerate to become less functional than they were at birth. There is every reason to suppose that the same thing happens within the human nervous system. Without input from the outside world, the brain will not grow. The characteristics of the inputs that produce growth are not well understood. It would seem, however, that light alone is not enough for the visual system; the light must be patterned. The same is probably true of the other senses.

It seems likely that a variety of developments contributes to increase the amount of information that can be processed. The process of habituation is almost certainly important in this change. Habituation, remember, involves the construction of an internal schema of any frequently occurring stimulus. The availability of a schema of any familiar stimulus seems to reduce the informational demands of that stimulus. The familiar does not preempt our attention in the same way that the completely unfamiliar does. Habituation to the sight of the hand may be responsible for the growth in information use seen in reaching. There is no doubt that infants, from birth on, do look at their hands a great deal. The fascination of the hand was brought home to me strongly when I saw a baby whose hands had been bandaged from birth. When the bandages were removed, at around three months, the hand captured the baby's visual attention totally. It was difficult to induce him to look at anything else for two days. Presumably it took this long to form a schema of the hand so that it did not preempt attention in the same highly demanding way.

If habituation is very important in early perceptual learning, it also seems true that learning what goes with what is equally important in simplifying the world of the child. There are a number of what-goes-with-what rules that we use to organize the world. One of them is often referred to as the *proximate organizing rule*. Stated as simply as possible, this rule says that contours close to one another, or closer than the average in a scene, are probably contours of a single object and so can be treated as one rather than two units. For example, (17) is clearly six rows of dots and is much easier to see than (18), where we cannot use the proximate organizing rule. It seems that babies have to learn the proximate organization of the world. For example, if babies are shown three dots, two close together and one peripheral, like so:

●　　●　●

they are surprised if any dot is put into motion. The measure used for gauging surprise was an abrupt change in the baby's sucking rate. Not until the age of nearly one year are babies more surprised by movement of one of the proximate dots than by movement of the peripheral dot. Movement of one of the proximate dots breaks what is, to us, a perceptual unit and so is more surprising than is movement of the dot that is a unit off by itself. Since

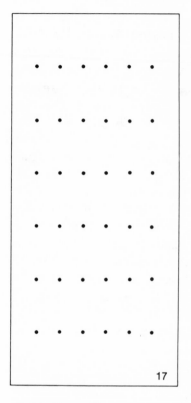 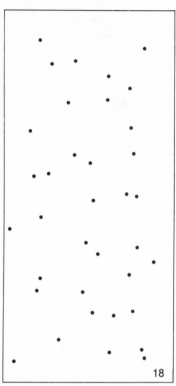

17, 18. *Figure 17 is easy to take in at a glance because the proximate organizing rule applies to let us see six rows of dots. Not so with Figure 18.*

babies of less than a year are not surprised by this change, we can surmise that they do not yet have the principle of proximity available to them to organize their world.

Some of the other what-goes-with-what rules are available at much earlier age. One rule, called *good continuation*, is used to organize contours that are broken by intervening objects: if the contours on each side of the break have the same direction, they should be treated as the same contour. Infants of eight weeks make use of this rule when shown a figure as unfamiliar to them as the triangle with a bar over it at the top of (19). Babies were trained to respond to this and were then shown the other figures in (19). Without exception they transferred their responses to the complete triangle, not to any of the nontriangles shown in (19). Since it is unlikely that the babies ever saw a complete triangle before the experiment, familiarity with triangles can hardly explain such behavior; application of the good continuation rule does. Only if the babies saw the broken contours of the original figure as a triangle would we expect them to transfer a learned response exclusively to the complete triangle in the way that they do.

The moral to be drawn from these experiments is reasonably clear. Although the infant has severe information-processing limits, he is also armed with a number of tricks for overcoming them. Some of these tricks, like the

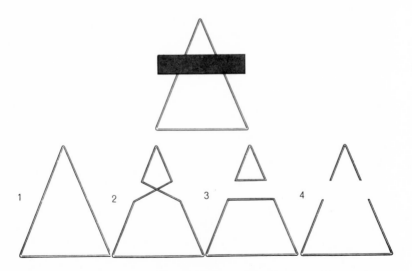

19. *We see the top figure as a triangle covered with a bar—like 1 rather than 2, 3, or 4. So does an eight-week-old baby.*

good continuation rule, may be inborn. Others, like habituation and the proximate organizing rule, depend upon experience. In either case, the effect is to allow the infant to ignore some of the recurring regularities in the environment and to concentrate his limited information-processing capacity on what is new and interesting.

5 / Adjustments to Growth

One of the most fascinating adjustments the baby must make is an adjustment to his own growth. Growth changes the baby's auditory perception, particularly auditory localization. It changes visual perception, perception of size, and the binocular detection of the position of objects. It must also, surely, create problems for the proprioceptive perception of position of body parts.

The development of accurate auditory localization has been studied, using reaching as an index of accuracy. Babies sit in a totally dark room. A noise-making object is introduced in one of several standard positions. The number of times the baby reaches is counted and, to yield an index of accuracy, compared with the number of times he actually touches the object. To make sure inaccuracy does not stem from having to reach in darkness, a separate control experiment is done. The babies are shown the same object, but it is noiseless and they are not allowed to reach for it until the lights have been switched off. The babies here are reaching in darkness to a place where they remember seeing an object. As far as reaching is concerned, the two situations are the same; the babies must reach for an object without being able to see their hands. Before the age of six months, auditorily guided reaching is more accurate than visual memory reaching for objects placed straight ahead of the baby, but much less accurate in the periphery, off the midline. Now this is about what we would expect, given the growth problems of the auditory system. There is no problem with sounds in the midline plane, because they arrive at both ears simultaneously. All other positions are specified by time differences that change as the baby grows, and it seems to take six months to learn to compute the value of these time differences.

The size problem for the eye is caused by eye's growth, which changes the size of the image produced by any object at a given distance. This affects accurate reaching and grasping. The eyes grow farther apart as the baby grows, with the result that a given object at a given distance will produce a smaller retinal image so that the object looks farther away than it really is, making location of it more difficult. However, the accuracy of a baby's grasping gets better and better as he becomes older. The way in which it is improved does not seem unduly mysterious. Babies are fascinated by their hands right from birth. They will sit or lie there changing their finger-thumb separations while looking at their hands. They tend to do this particularly while reaching, when the hand is in the same part of the visual field as an object. It is thus perfectly possible that the baby learns to match the seen size of objects to the seen size of his hand. This solution appears almost too simple to be true, but it does seem to account for the data.

Vision plays an important role in the resolution of proprioceptive problems. The fact that the baby learns to monitor his hand during the act of reaching permits him to make very accurate reaches. But it also allows him to forget about the proprioceptive specification of his hand position. The baby can find out where his hand is by looking at it, and there is some evidence that babies do come to rely on vision to locate their hands. The reaches of babies of four to six months are very direct: the hand is moved in a straight line from wherever it is to the location of the target. This direct reaching disappears over the next few months. What the baby then does, seemingly, is to stick his hand out into the visual field, check where it is by eye, and use his visual system to bring the hand to the object. There is some slight evidence that babies come to rely on this mechanism so completely that they can no longer make accurate reaches without visual guidance. If a baby of five months is shown an object and the lights are then switched off, so that he has to make his reach in the dark, he will still go pretty directly to the object. In the same circumstances an older baby does not reach out with the same accuracy. The hand goes out and moves back and forth in the correct plane until it contacts the object. Tactual information is used to guide the terminal grasping. It seems that older babies can no longer use direct proprioceptive information to guide their reaching, so reliant on vision have they become.

The step toward making vision the sense that determines hand position would seem to be a step away from the intersensory coordination described above. Certainly the intersensory coordination of older babies is less compulsive than that of younger babies. This shows up in an experiment on binocular coordination, where babies are presented with *virtual objects*—objects that are visible but not tangible. The apparatus shown in (20) will be familiar to anyone who remembers three-dimensional movies. Two projection lamps produce two oppositely polarized images on a screen. The baby wears 3-D goggles, which means that his right eye sees one image and his left eye the other. The result in perception is that the baby sees an object floating in empty space; it has all of the visible properties of an

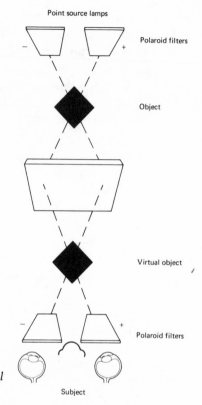

Point source lamps

Polaroid filters

Object

Virtual object

Polaroid filters

Subject

20. *A device for presenting virtual objects in empty air.*

object but, when the baby reaches out to grasp it, his hand will close on empty air. Babies of four to six months find this intensely surprising, but they do not seem to be able to do much about it. They keep reaching to the place where the object appears to be, acting very surprised each time but still compulsively trying to grab the object. There is a considerable change in the behavior of older babies, babies of eight or nine months. They will make a grab for the object too, but when the hand encounters only air, they do some interesting things. First of all they are likely to stare at their hand and then bang it on the nearest surface, for all the world as if they were trying to check out that the hand is working. They will then engage in a very prolonged visual inspection of the virtual object, often discovering that it is different from normal objects. The difference lies in what happens when the baby moves his head. Forever after the baby uses this difference in this situation to decide whether he is looking at a real object or a virtual object, reaching when presented with a real object, tending to giggle at the experimenter when presented with a virtual one. To me it looks very much as if the baby has succeeded in separating the perceptual world into a visual world and a tangible world. For younger babies the two are necessarily connected. Older babies live more and more in a world in which the information from the senses is separated into a visual world, an auditory world, and a tactual world. This shows in the virtual-object situation just described and in the auditorily guided reaching situation. The older baby is much less willing to reach for noise-making objects in darkness than the younger baby is. For the older infants sounds are for listening to, not for reaching for, a change that can have unfortunate consequences, as we shall see.

6 / Integrating Perception into Knowledge

Adults live in many worlds: a perceptual world, a world of the past, a world of the future, and a mediated world, available through TV, books, newspapers, and hearsay. Babies by contrast live in an immediate perceptual world, pretty much exclusively, little guided by memories or anticipations. Young babies can be enslaved by perceptual displays, stuck on them and stuck to them. Perception in young babies is not yet integrated into an overall context of behavior, and this integration is an essential part of perceptual development.

The process of habituation obviously serves to free the baby from attention to the increasingly familiar details of his environment. However, it is not for many months after the beginnings of habituation that he shows an ability to ignore new things that crop up while he is trying to do something else. An interesting behavioral trick of this sort is gaze aversion: a literal refusal to look at something, either because it is puzzling or because it is distracting. The latter motive is the more interesting for our purposes. Unfortunately, it is relatively unstudied. But one context where this kind of behavior has been noticed is reaching. Recall that babies of four to five months can be distracted from a reach by the sight of their hand in the visual field. Sometimes a baby at this point in development will look away from the object he is reaching for, presumably so that his hand can get unseen to the object. If this interpretation of the looking away is correct, it implies a rather developed integration of perception with behavior, a realization that an act may be disrupted by its perceptual consequences and an awareness of how to avoid these disruptions.

All of this seems very sophisticated. Unfortunately there are many other real-life situations where the baby does not seem able to call upon such resources. Rudolph Schaffer has remarked that babies are unable to restrain themselves from reaching out to grab any new object that is put before them.[1] Not until the last quarter of the first year will babies stop to take a good look at what is presented to them before reaching out to grab it. An amusing example of how nonfunctional this is was provided by Jerome Bruner.[2]

> Bruner gave a baby a toy. The baby took it. He then offered the baby another toy. The baby took it with his other hand. He offered the baby still another toy. If the baby was especially dextrous, he could grab this third one, while keeping a grip on the first two. At this point the baby is sitting like an overtrimmed Christmas tree, not really able to play with any of the three toys. Now comes the denouement. The baby is offered a fourth toy. Crash! The first three drop, any old where, as the baby compulsively reaches out to take the new thing on offer.

Older babies develop a more rational way of coping with situations like this, but it takes a long time.

The same sort of process may be involved in some aspects of the development of object permanence. The baby goes through several stages before he comes to believe that objects continue to exist even when they are no longer in sight. A natural situation is one in which, say, a ball rolls behind a chair. If the child retrieves the ball after its disappearance behind the chair, he must have some understanding of the ball's continuing existence which is not dependent upon his perception of it. A baby's growing ability to find an object that has been hidden can be tested by placing the object inside one of a set of other objects, with various odd permutations carried out to make the finding more difficult. At some point in this developmental sequence a baby will stop his search routine if he finds anything at all under any of the cups or cloths that have been used as hiding places. It doesn't matter how unlike the original target of the search the new object is. This could result from poor memory, or from the kind of distractability we have been talking about. This distractability is over by the time the baby is a year old. At this point and by some mysterious process, our infant begins to use his perceptual system, rather than being used by it. Internal memories and expectations control the baby's behavior, and he uses his perceptual system to realize these expectations.

Along with this kind of change goes a fascinating change in the status of perception within the hierarchy of systems that control the baby's behavior. We are all familiar with situations in which we refuse to believe our eyes, not accepting the evidence of our senses. We are not normally called upon to doubt our senses in any dramatic context. Most often it is an everyday situation where we are subjected to some illusion. The most dramatic instances come when we are watching a stage magician: we know that we are being deceived yet often cannot say why. There is a clear point in development when, it seems, the baby assumes a similar superior status in regard to the data provided by his senses. There is a developmental shift that results in babies, too, refusing to believe their eyes, when the visual evidence contradicts some internal knowledge about the world.

In one of my own investigations I used a device that

could make solid objects appear to fade away softly and silently, like puffs of smoke in the wind or banks of fog dissolving in a hot sun. This was achieved by a system of half-silvered mirrors that could be lit to show either an object or a blank space; the perceived change after a gradual change in the lighting was of an object slowly dissolving into nothing. My own older children referred to this device as a Boojum box. Nonetheless they were not the least afraid of the box and were quite happy to climb in and out of it. They "knew" that solid real objects do not dissolve like puffs of smoke. Babies acquire this knowledge toward the end of the first year of life. Faced with my box, young babies seemed to accept that the objects in question were gone. After the disappearance of the object they showed no further interest in the display. By the age of one year, this acceptance of visual input was over. The babies crawled up to the box, banged it, peered around it and then around the rest of the room until they found the object that had disappeared, at which point they would glare at me, expressing wordlessly the feelings of triumph they may well have been experiencing.

Distrust of the senses and reliance on other sources of knowledge grows during development. Indeed there is some evidence that the process goes so far that one can be led into illusions. Adults are quite susceptible to illusions produced by presenting odd-sized versions of familiar objects. An oversized chair will be as normal-sized and at a closer distance than it really is. A miniature Rolls-Royce is seen as normal-sized but at a greater distance than it really is. But children of up to five or six years of age will give a reasonable estimate of the true size and distance of the aberrant objects presented. Beyond this age they become as suspectible to the illusion as adults are.

Reliance on knowledge rather than on the immediate information from the senses is good policy in many more situations than it is not. Older children can use knowledge to overcome the built-in disabilities of the perceptual system in ways that younger children cannot. A simple demonstration of this is the horizontal-vertical illusion. A vertical line looks longer than a horizontal line that is actually of the same length. If you start with two horizontal lines both of the same length, and rotate one to the vertical position, you have put knowledge of the length before rotation in conflict with the immediate perception that the vertical line is longer. Children of up to six resolve the conflict in favor of perception and say that the vertical line *is* longer. Older children by contrast say that, although the vertical line *looks* longer, both are *really* the same.

This sophisticated separation of appearance and reality is a continuation of the initial separations made in infancy, and a separation that will continue throughout life. Much adult thought is about unseen and unseeable entities: for example, luck, God, responsibility. Any mental system that kept perception in the preeminent position that it occupies in the postnatal period would be quite incapable of coping with these fictive entitites. It has been argued that we would be happier and healthier if we stayed closer to the world of our senses. That might be so, but there is no way we shall ever know. The development away from perceptual preeminence seems universal, occurring in all cultures at all times.

7/ Learning To Use One's Senses

The perceptual system of the newborn grows more and more competent during the period of infancy. During this period of rapid growth the system is very susceptible to damage. Lack of environmental input, or a biased selection of environmental inputs, can destroy the structure that is present at birth.

The best evidence of this comes from studies of the fate of vision under conditions where the visual system cannot receive its appropriate inputs. Babies may be born with correctable visual defects, such as cataracts. Cataract is a condition in which the normally transparent lens of the eye becomes cloudy and nearly opaque, so that while diffuse light may reach the retina, no patterned or structured light can do so. The effect must be somewhat akin to looking through a frosted-glass door, seeing light and fluctuations in light, with no pattern at all. This condition can be corrected in various ways. The opaque lens can be removed. If contact lenses, or appropriate eyeglasses, are then applied, the condition is virtually cured, from an optical point of view. But the optical correction may come too late to be functional. If the condition is not corrected at an early age, it might as well not be corrected at all, at least in the vast majority of cases. The correction may be a technical success, an optical success, but a complete functional failure. Generally by the time a baby has lived six months, without benefit of patterned vision, it is too late to introduce patterned vision. The baby makes no use of the capacity at all.

Whether it is true to say that the baby does not do this or whether we should say that he cannot do it is a difficult question. The visual system continues to be susceptible to damage for some time. If one eye is damaged so that there is no binocular input, there may be permanent impairment of the binocular system, even if the period of monocular vision is as short as one week. This kind of suspectibility lasts into the third year of life. Even after vision has been used for some years, temporary impairment may result in a loss of capacity that is hard to reverse. Three classic cases of this kind were described by W. Uhthoff, who summed them up in the following way:

> the defect is purely cerebral in character . . . these young children have, as it were, forgotten how to see; and . . . at an age when, owing to their youth, the whole psycho-physical mechanism is still so little established, the deliberate exclusion—the suppression, almost—of visual sensation plays an important part in their sensory life.

He cites the following behavior:

> On being called to come, the child at first stands still; only when bidden more firmly does she begin to grope slowly forward, obviously directing herself by ear alone, though her eyes are wide open. Her line of advance is generally a wrong one, and she bumps into every obstacle.

And later:

> If a piece of sugar, which the child has a liking for, is thrown on the floor in front of her, so that she hears where it falls, she still does not look down at all, but gazes aimlessly straight ahead.

His patients were between two and a half and three and a half years of age. The maximum period without vision was six months, and this seemingly short period produced the drastic effects just described. Uhthoff described his patients as "forgetting how to see."[1] This may be an apt description for patients who have had vision for the first year or two of life. They can recover the use of their sight, can remember how to see, even after very long periods without vision.

There is evidence that a different and more destructive process may operate in those who are blind from birth. It appears that the areas of the brain normally available for vision may be taken over for other functions. This has been demonstrated for subfunctions within the visual systems of animals other than man. Within the visual system there are never cells that respond only to binocular input at birth. If one eye is covered, these binocular nerve cells are taken over by the uncovered eye and will in time become monocular nerve cells and will not respond to binocular stimulation. Similar things occur if there is restriction of input to one part of the retina. The normal projection from the eye to the brain is very orderly. If only a part of the eye is getting input, that part will take over other areas of the brain that were reserved for the unused portions of the eye. Once taken over, these areas cannot, it seems, be recaptured. It seems possible that complete loss of visual function in congential blindness is caused by a takeover of "visual" areas of the brain by the other sensory modalities, which *are* receiving inputs.

Blindness occurring later in development appears to have less drastic effects. If the condition is reversible, it is possible to restore visual function, although a process of relearning does seem to be necessary. However, the relearning process is partly a matter of changing a hierarchy of functions. A blinded individual can quickly come to rely on other senses. It is a matter of moving vision back up the hierarchy once it is restored.

It is a curious fact that individuals who have been sighted are better able to use their other senses for particular perceptual purposes than are the congenitally blind. Early visual awareness seems to create a knowledge of the structure of the world that cannot be given by other senses. In part this may result from the deficiency in the information coming from other senses. Audition, for example, is a very restricted spatial sense, as we shall see.

Thus far we have discussed perception and its development as an immediate process, whereby we respond to the part of the world around us that impinges on our sensory receptors. But perception is also the process whereby we get direct information about aspects of the world we cannot experience. We use our perceptual system to interpret representations of worlds we can never see. In the man-made world we live in, the perception of representations is as important as the perception of real objects. By a representation I mean any man-made stimulus array intended to serve as a substitute for a sight or sound that could occur naturally. Some representations are meant to be stimulus surrogates; to produce exactly the experience as the natural world would have done. The most common of these are high-fidelity stereophonic or quadrophonic music systems that aim to recreate the musical experience you would have in a concert hall or auditorium. *Trompe l'oeil* paintings and 3-D stereograms aim at a similar recreation of the exact experience that you would have if you were to be in the place where the painting or stereogram was made. Surrogates are in a sense irrelevant to the problem of perception of representations. Since a very good surrogate will produce the exact input that the real scene would, it is no wonder that we perceive what is represented. It would be more surprising if we did not. Even the best surrogates may require some learning before they can be fully enjoyed, however. Georg von Békésy recounted the tale of how in the early days of radio, when earphones were used to listen, an important political personage demanded to know why it was that when wearing earphones he heard voices in the middle of his head. The auditory information specified a sound source out there, but there was nothing visible out there. The politician's wife thought a visit to a psychiatrist as soon as possible the only answer, but Békésy managed to cure him without recourse to such a politically unfortunate step. This man had to learn to ignore the conflict between his eyes and his ears before he could enjoy the surrogate information entering his ears. Similar things happen to all of us. Even in live performances of music, the use of amplification systems means that we must reconcile the sight of the performer in one place with the source of his voice or guitar many feet away from him. Although most of us do this quite automatically, it is probable that children have to learn to ignore the conflicts between the stimuli if they are to enjoy fully the use of surrogates.

Representations that are not surrogates are more interesting and more common. Clearly a cube is represented in (21). It can be turned into a surrogate for a cube if one eye is closed and the drawing held exactly twelve inches in front of the open eye. However, even when it is not in this position, we can easily see that it is a cube, and we can use the representation for all sorts of purposes. Can children? How soon does a child become able to see that an object is a representation of some other object? How soon can he tell that marks on paper represent some other object? There

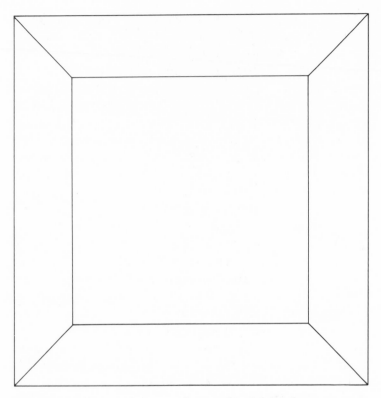

21. *Held exactly 8 inches from the eye, this drawing becomes a surrogate cube.*

is one important study that suggested that the ability to pick up the information in representations is innate and does not require learning. Julian Hochberg and Virginia Brooks took one normal child and prohibited pictures from his environment from birth on. When the child had developed a reasonably large vocabulary and could name many real-world objects, he was shown pictures of these objects and asked to name them. The pictures used are shown in (22). The child's naming was quite accurate.

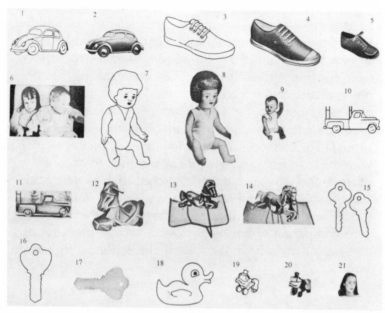

22. *A nineteen-month-year-old child who had never seen a picture of anything was able to name all the items in this array.*

Since the child had never been shown a picture before, and had never been taught to name pictured objects, the investigators concluded that the ability to perceive the significance of representations does not depend on prior experience and is therefore innate.[2] Is this strong conclusion correct? While I myself accept the results of the study as generally valid, even though only one child was involved, I think the conclusions are too strong. To understand my objections it will be necessary for us to take a detour and consider the processes of object identification per se.

The representations that we use in perceiving and remembering objects are general and abstract at all points in development. There are functional reasons why this is so. One purpose that is served by abstract internal representations is cross-modal recognition or comparison. Consider the following cross-modal experiment performed by Peter Bryant.[3] Eight-month-old babies were shown two objects, from the four shown in (23). They were shown that one object rattled and the other did not. The babies were then allowed to reach under a cover where the two objects had been placed. They succeeded in choosing the one that rattled. The converse case was to allow the babies to play with the toys without seeing them and then to show them the toys and see which one they picked. Babies were again successful in picking a rattle from a silent toy in this situation. There is no way they could have done this had they been comparing visual pictures with tactual impressions. The babies must have recognized the rattle as "rounded

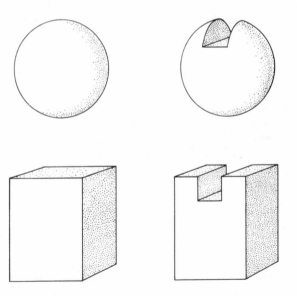

23. *Objects used in Peter Bryant's experiment. Babies of eight months who had seen these could afterward recognize them by touch, and vice-versa.*

with a piece cut out," a description that can be based on visual or tactual input equally well.

Abstract descriptions such as "rounded with a piece cut out" are commonly referred to as "distinctive features." It appears that our perceptual system operates with distinctive features rather than sense-specific items. One ingenious experiment demonstrating this was carried out by Anne Pick.[4] In her experiment, kindergarten children were trained to identify one letter-like form from among a number of others that differed from it in various distinctive features. A sample of the task is shown in (24), along with the list of distinctive features involved. The children learned to identify the standard form quite quickly and soon stopped confusing it with the others. When this point was reached, the children were split into two groups and given one of two similar tasks. One group went into an identification task just like the first, in which the correct form was the same one they had been working with before. However, the features that distinguished the standard from the other forms were totally different (25). The other group of children was asked to identify a totally different form (26). That form and the others it had to be discriminated from, however, were defined by the same distinctive features that had been in operation in the first learning experience. If we do in fact perceive in terms of distinctive features, we would expect this latter group of children to do very well on the second task, since it involved the same distinctive features that their perceptual system had become attuned to in the first task. This is just what happened. The children working with the same distinctive features did very much better than the children working with the same actual form and different distinctive features. This shows that perception does not operate with literal copies of inputs from the world. Rather, the

24, 25, 26. *Figures used in Anne Pick's experiment. We identify shapes by distinctive features that we abstract.*

perceptual system operates with the abstract distinctive features of the object itself.

What has this to do with a child facing his first picture? Any pictorial representation of an object must contain some of the distinctive features that allow you to identify an object. It need not have all of them but it must have enough, or else it would fail to be a pictorial representation at all. In that sense a pictorial representation is a partial surrogate of the object, rather than a pure representation. In fact, to the perceptual system of a child, a pictorial representation may be more of a surrogate than it is to an adult, because these are probably the distinctive features that define a real object. Their absence certainly signified something not real. Initially "not real" is the same as "not worth attending to." But this phase passes. Babies do start to attend to pictures and pictured objects. Still I have never seen a baby try to pick up a pictured toy, or eat a pictured cookie, or do anything else with the picture of an object that he might be expected to do with a real object. Pictures seem forever to be consigned to the limbo of the unreal.[5]

Somehow pictures must get from this unreal status to a position in which they can stand for the reality they represent. This is a considerable problem, despite the Hochberg and Brooks finding that a child would name a picture of an object by the same name he used for the object itself. All this means, I have argued, is that the same distinctive features elicit the same name in both situations, whether a real or a pictured object is presented. A child who can do this may still fail completely to comprehend a picture as a representation. This is brought out in a study done by Jane Dunkeld. She showed babies and young children life-size pictures of two cups. One cup was tilted so as to reveal a small piece of candy. The children were also shown two real cups identical with those in the picture, with the exception that the candy cup was not tilted so that the candy was invisible. The child's task, of course, was to find the candy. This task was amazingly difficult for the one- to two-year-olds in the study. The older children, who did succeed, did so by using language as an intermediary, or so it seemed. When shown the picture they would say to the world around, "The candy is under the spotty cup." When shown the real cups, they might spontaneously say, "Candy under the spotty cup," and go and pick up that cup. If they did not, one could probe them by asking "Where is the candy?" Their reply, "Under the spotty cup," would be enough to trigger a search under that cup.

This study suggests to me that language is required to mediate pictorial representation, at least initially. The child will not see one thing as standing for another—and that is the essence of representation—without the verbal link. Language is the most flexible system of representation that has been evolved. It predates pictorial representation by several millennia in human evolution. It should not be too surprising that verbal representation predates pictorial representation in the evolution of the individual child.

Recognizing that a picture can represent things is certainly quite different from being able to name the things in the picture. Some aspects of representation are quite as abstract and conventional as mathematical symbols. Representation of spatial relations is conventionalized in different ways in different societies. Compare the three different ways of representing perspective in (27). It is no wonder that children have to learn the meaning of representative conventions.

There is some evidence too that children have to learn to interpret the storyline in a picture book. This was brought home to me most forcibly by a study done by Ann Mayer some years ago. She presented children with a series of pic-

27. *Three ways of representing perspective. These ways are all widespread, and quite arbitrary.*

tures all containing a representation of the same dog. She asked the children to tell her a story about the dog. The children were able to say something about the dog in the first picture. When they went to the second picture, their almost invariable comment was "There's another dog." Their stories thus had no storyline at all. This situation was quite changed when the same pictures were given with the dog removed. The dog was given as a cutout that could be placed anywhere in any picture. This modification led to real stories with plots. Even in appreciating a simple storybook, then, there may be considerable problems to be overcome. It goes without saying that the abstract representations used by engineers or architects must be yet more difficult.

8 / Artificial Senses for Handicapped Children

One of the tragic problems of development arises whenever a child loses the use of a sense. The two most severe handicaps are blindness and deafness.

It is obviously very hard for a deaf baby to learn language. The deaf baby may babble away like a normal baby, but his babbling will not turn into articulated speech unless he can hear the sounds used by the speakers around him. Some cases of deafness can be helped simply by a hearing aid. Then the only requirement is early diagnosis, since too long without linguistic input may mean that language can never be acquired. If a hearing aid will not help a particular case of deafness, the problem is then to find ways of giving the child auditory information through his other senses. The most obvious sense to use might seem to be vision, which is by far the most complex and capable of the senses. It seems plausible that one should be able to feed auditory information through the eye, particularly if I am right in thinking that the perceptual system operates with abstract dimensions rather than sensorily specific dimensions.

Unfortunately, our ability to present auditory information in visual terms is very restricted. This is a matter of technology rather than principle. The machines we have, such as oscilloscopes and spectrographs, that convert auditory signals into visual displays do not present the displays in a way the eye can analyze. The dimensions of the visual displays are not the dimensions used by the visual system to analyze its inputs. It has proved difficult to train anyone to recognize a sound from its visual representation.

A more promising line of investigation was begun by Georg von Békésy.[1] Békésy won a Nobel Prize for his work on the ear. He noted that the snail-like shape of the cochlea of the ear was not necessary to its proper operation. The same function could be obtained if a model of the coiled cochlea were unrolled into a long tube. Békésy made such tubes and attached them to the forearms of his subjects. The resulting apparatus enabled the basic auditory information that comes into the ear as pressure variations on the cochlea to go into the forearm as pressure variations on its surface.

Békésy studied the ability of subjects to use these artificial ears. One of his surprising first results was that these devices could be used for auditory localization. After a little practice the subjects could locate sound sources by way of the time-of-arrival differences on their forearms. The sounds were felt to be "out there," not simply impressed on the surface of the skin. More complex discriminations are also possible. Similar devices are currently being used to teach language to deaf children—successfully, I am told.

The problems of the blind child are perhaps even more severe than those of the deaf. Lack of vision has profound consequences for development. The motor development of the blind deviates from that of sighted children. Perhaps because of this, their intellectual development is not the same as that of the sighted. Again, for perhaps related reasons, their personalities may develop in ways different from those of sighted children, as we will see. These differences are all due to the inability of other senses to provide the information that vision normally provides. Finding the cause of the differences is theoretically important because it allows us to define the role of vision in normal development. Also, by finding out what it is that vision normally provides and the other senses do not, we can hope to change the information provided by the other senses and perhaps in this way give the blind baby substitute eyes.

The schedules of development for blind and sighted babies are shown in (28).[2] There are only two sorts of item that really differentiate between them: reaching and independent walking. Blind babies are very late in learning to reach for noise-making objects. It has even been reported

Item	Median Age (in months)		Difference
	Sighted	Blind	
Elevates self by arms, prone	2.1	8.75	6.65
Sits alone momentarily	5.3	6.75	1.45
Rolls from back to stomach	6.4	7.25	0.85
Sits alone steadily	6.6	8.00	1.40
Raises self to sitting position	8.3	11.00	2.70
Stands up by furniture	8.6	13.00	4.40
Stepping movements (walks hands held)	8.8	10.75	1.95
Stands alone	11.0	13.00	2.00
Walks alone, 3 steps	11.7	15.25	3.55
Reaching, audible object	n.a	11.00	6.00
Reaching, visible object	5.0	n.a.	

28. *Schedules of development for blind and sighted babies.*

that some of them never attain that skill. Independent locomotion, walking without a human guide, is even more difficult.

It is a bit misleading to compare such schedules. The conditions of testing are not the same, of course, since the sighted babies can use vision and the blind babies cannot. If the sighted babies are tested in darkness, their apparent advantage disappears. Consider the development of reaching for noise-making objects. Early on there is no difference between blind and sighted babies in much of the perceptual-motor behavior I have described. Blind babies even stare at their hands, tracking them with their unseeing eyes. Not surprisingly they also turn their eyes toward a sound source and will extend their hand to grasp it. Sighted babies tested in darkness behave in exactly the same way. They look at their hands, turn toward sound sources, and reach out to grasp at the sound. Reaching for a noise-making object becomes quite accurate by the age of six months. However, the probability of a baby's doing so declines sharply at around this time. Sounds are to be heard, not reached for or looked at. This is true for both the blind and the sighted baby. After this, it is difficult ever again to get any baby, blind or not, to reach for an unseen, noise-making object. What we have to explain, therefore, is why sounds stop signifying the presence of graspable objects between birth and six months.

There are a variety of possible explanations. The first is that processes in the brain—normal, immutable results of growth—produce the dissociation. If this explanation is true, nothing can be done to alleviate the lot of the blind child because nothing will induce him to treat sound as a source of information about objects. However, the causes of the six-month-old's dissociation of sound and object may be functional, not physical. If functional explanations prove correct, it would open up the possibility of intervention on behalf of the blind child. One of the possible functional explanations stems from the limited information in the sounds emitted by noise-making objects. Adults and babies can register the position of sounds to right or left by utilizing time-of-arrival differences at the ears. This is one kind of information that is available in sounds emitted by objects. But let us look at the information that is not given by such sound sources.

First, there is no way of telling instantly from the sound alone whether a sound source is in front of us or behind us (29). For adults this ambiguity is not serious because it can be resolved by a head movement; infants are less able to make such movements. Blind babies in particular have no way of visually checking where a sound source is. Second, there is a lack in the output from sound sources of any information about up-down or "azimuth" position. There is considerable controversy among those who work in this field over whether or not adults can pick up azimuth position without head movements of the sort shown in (30). With such head movements, there is no difficulty, but head movements are a problem for babies. Third, there is no information given by sound sources about distance. It is impossible for anyone to tell how far away a sound source is. Even judgment of the distance of familiar noise-making objects is little better than guesswork in adults. Fourth, there is nothing in a sound to specify what sort of object is emitting the sound. Take an obvious example, the human voice. This could come from a human face, a television set, a hi-fi speaker, a portable radio. Only the last of these is really a graspable object for a baby. Finally, few objects in the world actually emit sounds. The baby, blind or sighted, will continually encounter objects that do not make noises.

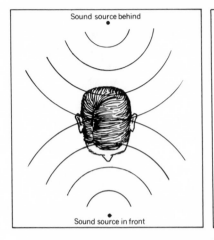
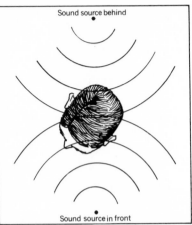

29. *As the drawing on the left shows, there is no difference in time of arrival at the ears between a sound from in front and a sound from behind. Only by a head movement that maximizes time differences (as on the right) can the sound source be located.*

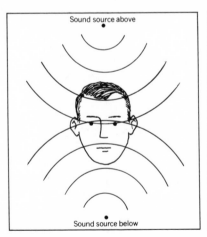
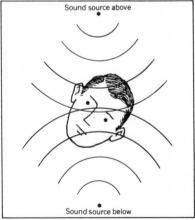

30. *Sounds from directly above or below can likewise only be located by a head movement.*

Let us put all of this in a strictly functional context. Suppose a blind baby is willing and able to reach out and grasp noise-making objects. He can tell whether an object is in his midline plane or on his right or his left. When the noise comes in, suppose it specifies an object in the midline plane. The sound cannot tell him whether the object is straight in front or straight behind, up or down, near or far. If it is a continuous sound, the baby has some chance of figuring out the first two of these dimensions. The last is impossible. If the sound source is not continuous, permitting the use of monitored head movements, the first two dimensions are out, perceptually, as well. Suppose the baby then reaches out. What are his chances of getting the sound source? It must be admitted that they are very, very slight. The baby, blind or sighted, can have no precise built-in knowledge about left-right or azimuth position, no precise information about distance or the length of his own arm. Left-right, up-down, front-back, near-far, and arm length must all be precisely specified for accurate reaching to occur. The sighted child who reaches and misses can *see* why he has missed. He can see his hand pass above or below, before or beyond the object of interest. The sighted child thus has correction possibilities that are not open to the blind child. On any functional account, behavior as unsuccessful as reaching for unseen noise-makers, behavior where even the source of error can hardly be detected, should simply fade out and die away, which is just what happens.

There is another more subtle problem raised for the blind child by the presentation of noise-making objects. To understand it we must consider an experiment done not on babies, but on animals. The experiment was one of many carried out by Richard Held.[3] The protagonists in the experiment were kittens who were connected together by the apparatus shown in (31). One kitten, the active kitten,

31. *Richard Held's apparatus. The kitten in the gondola can see as much as his companion, but he cannot act in a visual context.*

could move voluntarily anywhere within the limits of the apparatus. If he saw something interesting, he could move toward it. If he saw something unpleasant, he could move away. This kitten could use visual stimulation to control his movements and could use his movements to control the input coming to his eyes. The kitten encased in the gondola had no such interactive relationship with his visual world. He could not walk around or even touch the ground with his feet. The passive kitten saw only what the active kitten allowed him to see. When the kittens were removed from the apparatus and given a series of visual tests, the active kitten was essentially normal. The passive kitten, by contrast, simply did not react to visual inputs. He could see; his visual system was normal; but he had lost the capacity to act in a visual context. Forced to be passive in the experimental situation, he had become passive in all situations.

Now consider the situation of the blind baby. The auditory stimulation he gets is delivered to him by others. The baby does not determine what stimulation he gets, cannot shut his ears if he dislikes it, or make it continue if it is pleasant. With the sounds produced by noise-making objects, the blind baby is in exactly the same situation as the passive kitten was in Held's experiment. Is it any wonder, then, that the blind baby is unresponsive in the face of auditory stimuli that are thrust on him from outside?

At this point it is worth mentioning an observation frequently made about the temperament of blind babies. They are very "good" babies, quiet, undemanding, even-tempered—in a word, passive. Is it too much to suppose that the sensorimotor passivity spreads to become a generalized personality characteristic, a generalized attitude toward the world, an habitual learned helplessness?

All of the above applies to one class of auditory stimulation that comes from noise-making objects. There is a whole class of auditory stimulation that does not suffer from any of these limitations: the stimulation that comes from echoes. Suppose we make a noise by snapping our fingers. The sound waves produced by that noise radiate out from our hand and bounce back from any object in their path. The echoes produced in this way contain a great deal of information that sounds emitted by objects do not. The first and most important dimension discoverable from echoes is distance. Since sound travels at a constant speed, the farther away an object is, the longer will the echo it reflects take to reach the ear. The relationship is a perfectly predictable one, and a better indicator of distance than any visual stimulus. Second, echoes specify the direction of objects. The echo from an object on the right reaches the right ear before the left ear, and vice-versa, just as sound waves emitted from an object do. The echo does not specify up-down position, but it can specify the size of an object. The larger an object is, the more of the sound wave it will reflect back. This relation, in conjunction with distance specification, permits accurate determination of size at any distance. Echoes can even specify, to some extent, the shape of an object, although the specification is not at all precise.

What is the relevance of echoes to blind babies? It has been known for many years that those blind adults who are mobile use echoes to get the information they use in navigating the world. They use echoes from their footsteps, echoes from a tapping cane, echoes made by snapping their fingers, and so on. Echoes of this sort are not always available, and in recent years there has been a great deal of research on the utility of artificial echo-location devices, some of which seem to be very precise.

Let us assume that a blind baby could use echoes. What opportunity would he get to use them? In a normal Western environment, I'm afraid he would not have much opportunity at all. The baby cannot produce echoes by tapping his heel or snapping his fingers. The only source spontaneously available to him is his voice. But the usual environment will not be quite enough, or have the sort of furnishings, to allow registration of these echoes. In a typical Western home, with TV, radio, sound-absorbent carpets, and so on, there is not much opportunity to use the kinds of echoes a baby can produce. The subtle information in the echoes will be swamped by the overall ambient noise. Does this matter? Is there any evidence that babies, blind or sighted, can use echoes?

In the case of one blind baby there is some evidence. I was fortunate enough to be allowed to test this infant when his age was sixteen weeks (ten weeks premature, he was maturationally equivalent to a six-week-old normal baby). His behavioral repertoire was quite large. His vocalizations were strange, too, in that he produced an inordinate number of sharp, clicking noises with his lips and tongue. I had never heard a sighted baby make such noises, and guessed that they were intended to produce echoes. To test this, I dangled a large ball in front of the baby, completely silently. The baby turned to "look" at it. I moved the ball, again silently. After a vocalization interval of clicks, he turned to follow it. This performance was repeated seven times. All of the movements of the ball were completely quiet. The performance was spectacular enough for one member of the audience to be moved to doubt that diagnosis of blindness. Another produced the echo-location explanation. It seemed clear that this baby could use echoes.

The echo-location idea was explained to the baby's parents, and they were asked to make sure he had an opportunity to continue to make use of the ability. They did this by arranging toys over his crib. The position of the toys was changed every time the baby was put in. All of the toys were noise-makers of some sort and would make a sound when struck or pulled. The baby quite quickly learned that when he was put in his crib there would be a toy somewhere for him to play with. However, the only way he could find it would be to use echoes. By the age of sixteen weeks he could reliably find any largish object dangled over his crib, and he was able to generalize this ability to other situations to some extent.

At the age of sixteen weeks the baby was equipped with a very sophisticated echo-location device. This device produces echoes from objects as small as a knitting needle. In (32) a baby is seen wearing the device, which has a range of two meters over an eighty-degree field in front of the child. Any object in this range produces an echo, which is converted to audible frequencies by means of transducers. Distance is conveyed by the pitch of the signal, and size by the amplitude. The device operates continuously without requiring activity of the baby, so that he is free to use his vocalizations for other purposes. We hope that this machine will provide a substitute for vision in this child.

Fortunately, blindness and deafness are comparatively rare handicaps for a child. But the predicaments of the blind or deaf child can point up dangers that the normal child also faces. One of these is overstimulation. Amount

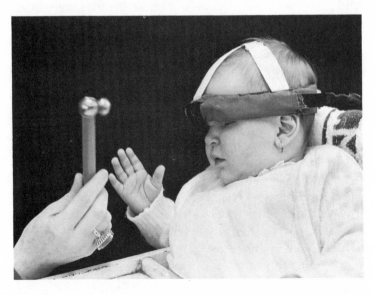

32. *The echo-location device.*

of stimulation has been the subject of an experimental study, carried out with human infants.[4] The study focused on babies growing up in a rather old-fashioned institution. As the authors describe it, it was an old building with old furniture. The babies lay in cribs, hollowed with use, which restricted their freedom of movement. The cribs were lined to prevent the babies from seeing one another. The ceilings were rather high, too, so that there was almost nothing for them to look at. Such conditions, of course, are criminally impoverished and represent misinformed views of the environment suitable for babies. Any amelioration brought about by the researchers was almost bound to improve the workhouse conditions the babies would have lived in without the intervention.

The most stimulated group of infants in the study were picked up and handled more often, the crib liners were removed, and the babies were given a multicolored stabile and patterned sheet to look at. These luxuries were introduced when the babies were thirty-seven days old. They were not totally appreciated. These babies cried more than control babies simply left in the barren institutional environment, and they were also less attentive to visual events in their environment. It seemed that too much had been introduced too soon, with the result that these babies avoided a world suddenly too complex. I cannot help thinking that it was the thirty-seven days in the institution prior to the introduction of these minor modifications that caused the babies to react so negatively. For the modifications *were* minor in terms of a normal home environment; only in terms of the impoverished institutional conditions could they have been disruptive. Nonetheless, given that all the babies in this study were deprived, it seems that too much input too quickly can create developmental problems for the baby. Anyone who wants to design an optimal environment for a developing baby will probably have to be guided by the baby. Too much stimulation is as bad as too little. A bored baby is as bad to live with as a switched-off baby. Programming the perceptual inputs of a child is the responsibility of that child's parents, and it is a considerable one. The average child needs more than the average parent thinks he does—but he has his limits. So long as this is realized, nothing but good can come from augmentation of the perceptual world of a child.

9/ Perception and Development

It is now time to sum up this brief review of the perceptual world of the child and to place perception in the overall context of human development. At the outset, we looked at the wonderful perceptual capacities of the newborn baby. In later chapters we looked at the ways in which these capacities change. Is there any general description of these changes that we can give?

Although any truly general characterization must be controversial, I propose to offer one anyway: the perceptual capacities of the newborn are very general or abstract; perceptual development consists in the ever-increasing specification of these abstract capacities. What does this mean in concrete terms? An obvious example comes from the study of the growing child's changing sensitivity to speech sounds. The newborn can segment the sounds of any language into the basic units of that language. He is ready for all possible languages. Soon, though, a child becomes set for the sounds of the language community he lives in. He begins to lose the capacity to respond to any language, a price that must be paid for the growing capacity to differentiate the sounds and sound chains of the language he hears every day. This is a clear example of the way in which a general capacity changes to become more and more specific.

A less obvious but perhaps more telling example comes from the study of the blind child who was fitted with a device that fed him spatial information through his ears. The presence of an object in the field of the device was signaled by a noise coming in through his ears. If the object moved toward him, the pitch of the noise changed, as did its amplitude. Within a few seconds of putting the device on, the baby knew that these changes signified the approach of an object toward his face. The important point is that no baby had ever before been presented with this kind of *specific* information. The sighted child in the same situation sees a complex of visual changes which, at an abstract level, are quite like the changes produced by the sonic device. It seems that the perceptual system is ready to use this kind of abstract information, regardless of the specific sensory modality by which it is presented. This readiness does not last long. In the first year or so the perceptual system gets used to a specific kind of input. This must be why operations to restore sight to the child born blind become less and less profitable as the child grows older.

The perceptual system, then, becomes more and more specified in the course of development. It operates within a more restricted range of stimulation but with a compensating increase in efficiency, making ever more refined and precise discriminations.

What is the place of perceptual development in the overall framework of human development? As I have tried to show, perception becomes less and less important as we grow. The information provided by our senses stays relatively constant throughout development. The way we interpret it changes. Consider disappearance transitions. Objects can disappear in many ways, sometimes incomprehensibly. We have no idea where the object has gone. Disappearances like this are the whole basis of conjuring tricks. Note, though, that while we adults suffer, or enjoy, the illusions that a conjurer produces, we know perfectly well that what we are seeing are illusions and that reality is different. The baby is affected by disappearance transitions in the same way, but he does not know that reality is different. This is something he has to learn, and, as far as we know, he learns it in the course of the first year of life. Later in development there are similar changes in the reliance we put on our senses, changes concerning what is called conservation. In (33) we see a full bottle of a soft

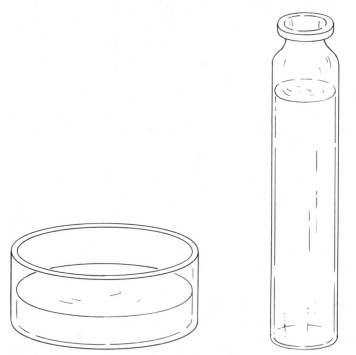

33. *The bottle and the glass actually contain the same amount, though they do not appear to. Pouring the drink from one to the other will convince an adult that this is so, but it will not convince a child under six: he sticks to the evidence of his senses.*

drink, along with the same amount of the liquid in a glass. It looks as if there is far more in the bottle than in the glass. Nonetheless we accept that the amounts are the same if we have seen the contents of the bottle poured into the glass. A child under six doesn't accept this. For him there is less in the glass than in the bottle. He allows the evidence of his senses to dominate his judgment. In time, the child stops making this error. In time, too, we rely less and less on what we can see to explain what we can see. We explain our world in terms of unseeable, imperceptible events and forces. And yet our perceptual world, the source of all we know, still conditions and shapes the way we know, even when we are reasoning in terms of the unseen and the imperceptible. Recall the famous debate in physics between those who thought of light as a shower of pebbles and those who thought of it as waves in a pool. At a theoretical level there is no difference between the conceptualizations. Translated into perceptual terms, they seemed so incompatible that physicists argued the issue for decades. A theory can be intellectually compelling, and yet we feel more comfortable if we can see some evidence that it is right—hence the enormous investments in bubble chambers, electron microscopes, and the like, which are made by modern science.

The more we grow away from the perceptual world, the more we are compelled to return to primitive certainties of perception.

References
Suggested Reading
Index

Credits

References

3 Perceiving Things, Perceiving People

1. J. B. Watson, *Psychology from the Standpoint of a Behaviorist* (Philadelphia: Lippincott, 1919).
2. M. Wertheimer, "Psychomotor Coordination of Auditory-Visual Space at Birth," *Science*, 1961, *134*, 1692.
3. E. R. Siqueland and L. P. Lipsitt, "Conditioned Head-Turning in Human Newborns," *Journal of Experimental Child Psychology*, 1966, *3*, 356-376.
4. G. Carpenter, "Mother's Face and the Newborn," in R. Lewin, ed., *Child Alive* (New York: Doubleday, 1975).

6 Integrating Perception into Knowledge

1. H. R. Schaffer, *The Growth of Sociability* (Harmondsworth: Penguin, 1971).
2. J. S. Bruner, *Processes of Cognitive Growth: Infancy* (Barre, Mass.: Barre Publishing, 1968).

7 Learning To Use One's Senses

1. W. Uhthoff, "Sitzungsber d. Marb Gesellschaft," 1892. Quoted in M. von Senden, ed., *Space and Sight* (Glencoe, Ill.: Free Press, 1960).
2. J. Hochberg and V. Brooks, "Pictorial Recognition as an Unlearned Ability: A Study of One Child's Performance," *American Journal of Psychology*, 1962, *75*, 624-628.
3. P. E. Bryant, P. Jones, V. Claxton, and G. M. Perkins, "Recognition of Shapes across Modalities by Infants," *Nature*, 1972, *240*, 303-304.
4. A. D. Pick, "Improvement of Visual and Tactual Form Discrimination," *Journal of Experimental Psychology*, 1965, *69*, 331-339.
5. T. G. R. Bower, "The Object in the World of the Infant," *Scientific American*, 1971, *225*(4), 30-38.

8 Artificial Senses for Handicapped Children

1. G. von Békésy, *Sensory Inhibition* (Princeton, N. J.: Princeton University Press, 1967).

2. From S. Faiberg and N. Bayley, "Gross Motor Development in Infants Blind from Birth," *Child Development*, 1974, *45*, 114-126.
3. R. Held, "Plasticity in Sensory-Motor Systems," *Scientific American*, 1965, *213*(5), 84-94.
4. B. L. White, *Human Infants: Experience and Psychological Development* (Englewood Cliffs, N.J.: Prentice-Hall, 1971).

Suggested Reading

T. G. R. Bower, *Development in Infancy* (San Francisco: Freeman, 1974). A more detailed and technical treatment of many of the experiments and findings referred to in this book.

E. J. Gibson, *Principles of Perceptual Learning and Development* (New York: Appleton-Century-Crofts, 1969). A text for serious students describing the classic issues in perceptual learning and development. It gives an exhaustive review of the data available up to 1966 or so, but has not been outdated by any subsequent discoveries.

Ernst H. Gombrich, *Art and Illusion* (Princeton: Princeton University Press, 1961). Gombrich has written several books on visual thinking. All of them are clear and full of fascinating insights into the ways in which perception structures our world.

Richard L. Held, *Perception: Mechanisms and Models. Readings from* Scientific American (San Francisco: Freeman, 1971). A collection of original articles on perception and perceptual development. The authors, many of whom I have cited earlier in this book, explain their studies clearly and nontechnically.

Index